ONE HUNDRED AND FIFTY YEARS OF LONDON FIRE BRIGADE IN PICTURES

Credits and acknowledgements

Written by London Fire Brigade Museum curators,
Jane Rugg and Elena Lewendon.

Designed by Chris Davies.

With special thanks to Terry Jones and Murray Beale.

This book is published with the kind support of
Bristol Uniforms Ltd, Mary Evans Picture Library
and Tradewinds.

All profits from this book will go to the following charities:
Burns Camps, Children's Burns Trust, Children of Fire,
RAFT, Restore, The Firefighters Charity.

First published 2015 by London Fire
and Emergency Planning Authority.
169 Union Street, London SE1 0LL.
london-fire.gov.uk

ISBN 978-0-9934205-0-4

Printed in United Kingdom by Tradewinds.

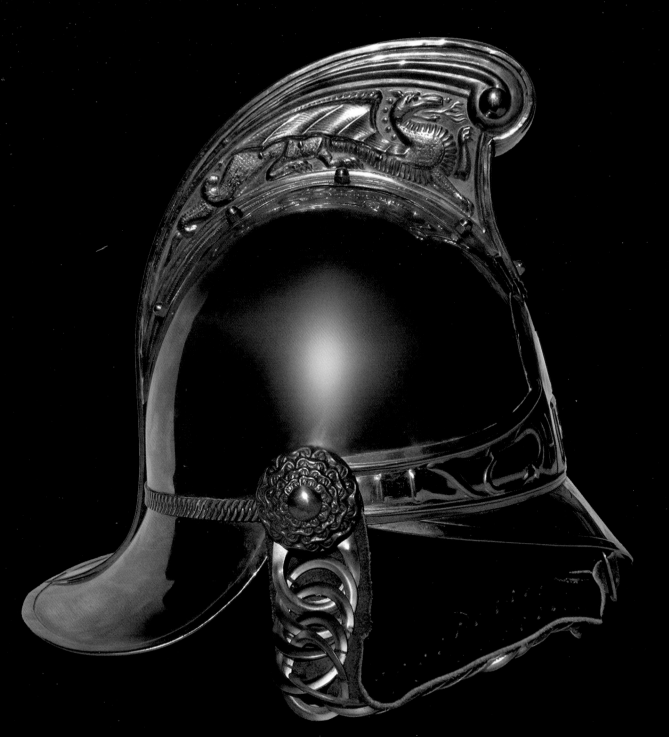

Contents

The 150th anniversary of London Fire Brigade is a momentous occasion that deserves celebration. The 150 photographs in this book chart some of the Brigade's achievements, commemorate the sacrifices made by the people who have served it and illustrate how the service has evolved over the last 150 years. It gives an insight into how the Brigade works every day to make London a safer place and takes a look at the people behind the uniforms.

Since the Metropolitan Fire Brigade began operating on 1 January 1866 the role of the fire service in London has changed dramatically, through peacetime and during war. Our responsibilities have evolved and so have the skills and capabilities within the Brigade.

London Fire Brigade not only fights fires but works proactively to prevent them happening in the first place. We work closely with the communities we serve to achieve this. We work with younger people through our youth schemes and with other public bodies to protect the most vulnerable people in society from fire. This pays dividends. To the great credit of all London Fire Brigade staff, the number of fires in London are the lowest they have been since records began.

It is a great honour to be Commissioner in the year that the Brigade celebrates its 150th anniversary. I am incredibly proud to be part of London Fire Brigade and equally proud of the staff, past and present, who make London Fire Brigade a world class fire and rescue service.

Ron Dobson CBE QFSM FIFireE
London Fire Commissioner

1860s 1870s 1880s 1890s 1900s 1910s 1920s 1930s

1865: Act of Parliament forming the Metropolitan Fire Brigade (MFB).

1866: MFB begins operation.

1866: Sir Captain Eyre Massey Shaw becomes Chief Officer.

1867–68: Iconic brass helmets introduced.

1867: MFB takes over the duties of the Royal Society for the Protection of Life from Fire.

1871: Pantechnicon warehouse fire.

1878: MFB headquarters moves from Watling Street to Southwark.

1878: Shaw publishes *Fire Protection*.

1878: Shaw publishes *Fires in Theatres*.

1880: Street fire alarms introduced.

1882: Alhambra Theatre Fire.

1889: London County Council takes over MFB.

1891: Shaw retires and is replaced by James Sexton Simmonds.

1891: Pensions are introduced.

1896: Commander Lionel De Latour Wells becomes Chief Officer.

1897: Cripplegate fire destroys 100 buildings in the City.

1899: Firefighters no longer recruited exclusively from the Royal Navy.

1900: Launch of Alpha II fireboat.

1902: Queen Victoria Street fire leads to hook ladders being introduced.

1902: Wells retires and is replaced by Rear Admiral James De Courcy Hamilton.

1904: MFB changed to London Fire Brigade.

1904: First motorised fire engine introduced.

1909: Hamilton

1914: Outbreak of the First World War.

1914: Defence of the Realm Act passed.

1918: Fire and collapse at Albert Embankment.

1918: Sladen retires and is replaced by Arthur Reginald Dyer.

1920: A two watch system is introduced.

1921: The last horses used at Kensington Fire Station are retired.

1933: Dyer retires and is replaced by Major Cyril Clark Boville Morris.

1935: Massey Shaw fireboat is launched.

1937: LFB headquarters moves from Southwark to Lambeth.

1938: Fire Brigade's Act formally establishing the Auxiliary Fire Service.

1938: Commander Sir Aylmer Newton George Firebrace becomes Chief Officer and in

1940s 1950s 1960s 1970s 1980s 1990s 2000s 2010s

1940: Operation Dynamo.

1940: The London Blitz begins.

1941: National Fire Service is formed.

1944: V1 and V2 attacks on London.

1945: Second World War ends.

1948: National Fire Service is denationalised.

1948: Sir Frederick William Delve becomes Chief Officer.

1949: The Auxiliary Fire Service re-established.

1949: Fire at Covent Garden Market.

1951: Broad Street fire.

1954: All new fire engines become diesel powered.

1957: Lewisham train crash.

1958: Smithfield Market fire.

1958: Street fire alarms are abolished.

1962: Delve retires and is succeeded by Leslie William Thomas Leete as Chief Officer.

1962: Blue lights are introduced on fire engines.

1965: Greater London Council (GLC) created.

1966: LFB celebrates its centenary.

1967: Hither Green rail crash.

1968: Auxiliary Fire Service disbanded.

1969: Dudgeon's Wharf explosion.

1970: Leete retires and is replaced by Joseph Milner.

1971–72: HAZCHEM system is designed and implemented.

1974: Green watch is created.

1974–75: Compressed air breathing apparatus introduced.

1975: Moorgate tube disaster.

1976: Milner retires and is replaced by Sir Peter Howard Darby.

1977: National Firefighters' strike.

1980: Darby is replaced by Ronald Alfred Bullers.

1982: Sue Batten becomes London's, and Britain's, first female firefighter.

1984: Salvage Corps disbanded.

1986: GLC abolished, London Fire and Civil Defence Authority (LFCDA) established.

1987: King's Cross Underground Station fire.

1987: Bullers is succeeded by Gerald Dawson Clarkson.

1988: Clapham rail disaster.

1991: Clarkson retires and is replaced by Brian Gordon Robinson.

1997: Dräger PA94 Plus model breathing apparatus is introduced.

1999: Introduction of the Inferno fire uniform.

1999: Paddington rail disaster.

1999: New fireboats Firedart and Fireflash become operational.

2000: LFCDA changes to London Fire and Emergency Planning Authority (LFEPA).

2000: Odin, the first fire investigation dog, is recruited.

2002: High specification chemical protection suits introduced.

2003: Robinson retires and Sir Ken Knight becomes new London Fire Commissioner.

2005: 7/7 London bombings.

2007: Ron Dobson replaces Knight.

2007: The Queen opens new headquarters at Union Street.

2010: Introduction of new PPE, including Gallet F1 helmets.

2012: Olympic and Paralympic Games hosted by London.

2012: World Rescue Challenge hosted by LFB.

2013: Helicopter crash in Vauxhall.

2014: Plane crash training exercise in East London.

2016: LFB celebrates 150th anniversary.

A fireman, to be successful, must enter buildings; he must get in below, above, on every side, from opposite houses, over brick walls, through panels of doors, through loop holes, through sky lights, through holes cut by himself in the gates, the walls and roof; he must know how to reach the attic from the basement by ladders placed on burnt half stairs and the basement from the attic by rope made fast on a chimney. His whole success depends on him getting in and remaining there, and he must always carry his appliances with him as without he is of no use."

Extract from *Fires and Fire Brigades* by Captain Sir Eyre Massey Shaw, 1889

Life at a fire station

"A fireman is always on duty... day or night he must be ready to answer the electric bells. He lives whether single or married, in the station and must not go out of the hearing of the bells without permission, taking turns to be downstairs all night fully dressed to go with the motor escape to be out of the station in 15 to 30 seconds. If any of you want to know what it is like, try, on a cold bitter night, to dress, get downstairs and out of doors in that time and, two or three minutes later, crawling on your hands and knees into a large warehouse filled with dense smoke."

Superintendent Albert Edward Edmonds, 1920s

Brixton Fire Station, 1890
Firefighters worked 24 hours a day and lived at fire stations with their families. Some fire stations were five or six stories high to accommodate all of the families. Every two years firefighters moved to a different station so they could experience other areas and fire risks.

Nov 3rd 1874 ... causing annoyance in the Station by quarrelling & fighting with his wife at 4—0. Pm of the 3rd Inst also in allowing his children to be about the Station in a dirty state ...

Above: William Walker, disciplinary – arguing with wife and children, 1874

Firefighters' leave was granted at the goodwill of their station officer and was dependent on the number of fires occurring. If a firefighter returned late from their leave they would be fined. When recruitment first began for the Metropolitan Fire Brigade over a thousand people were waiting to join. However, with the long hours, lack of pensions and little free time, many men began to leave the Brigade after just a few months of employment.

Right: A London fire station, 1900s

The Chief Officer, Captain Sir Eyre Massey Shaw, was inspired by the use of poles in American fire houses and their impact on improving response times. During the later half of the 19th century brass poles were fitted to fire stations.

Opposite page: London firefighters with their station pets, 1904

Firefighters kept pets at the fire station including dogs, cats, parrots and even monkeys.

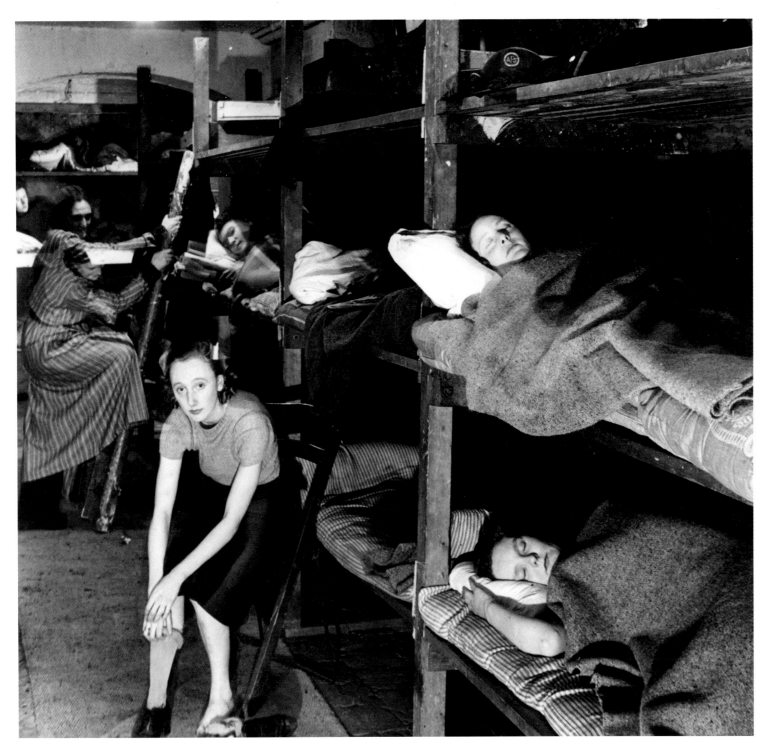

Left: Southwark Fire Station c.1940
In London there were about 300 substations for use during the war, these were mainly schools, garages and small factories which were adapted for the fire service. However, not all substations were changed and conditions were sometimes poor. Once the Blitz began, many members of the Auxiliary Fire Service slept at the fire station even when they were off duty to ensure they were available to help.

Right: Firefighters with their dog mascot, 1940s
During the war animals were kept at fire stations as pets. Some stations had pigs and chickens and grew their own vegetables in sandbags as part of the war effort to supplement their rations.

Above: Firefighters lending a helping hand, *c.*1943
Towards the end of the war, firefighters took up light industrial work at stations to help with the war effort. This included the production of equipment such as fire extinguishers, parachute containers and light bench work. During quieter times, Blitz artists and poets, commissioned by the War Office, and those working in the fire service took to painting and writing about their experiences.

Above: An appliance bay in a London fire station, *c.*1960s
The London County Council fire stations of the 1960s had a sleek modern design. These new post war stations included dormitories for night shifts because firefighters no longer lived at fire stations with their families. Poles continued to be used to ensure speedy response times.

Right: Eltham Fire Station, 1974
Although firefighters' families had not lived at fire stations for over 50 years, fire stations still provided a strong community presence, hosting open days, birthday parties and children's Christmas parties.

Schools engagement event, 2011
Fire stations continue to host open days and participate in community events and projects, including raising money for charity. The Brigade also works with local schools, promoting fire safety messages.

Horses

The Stables Knightsbridge L.F.B. Station.

Left: Knightsbridge Fire Station, *c*.1900s

Horses were used by London Fire Brigade to pull manual pumps, steam fire engines and wheeled escape ladders to a fire. The majority of the horses were on hire from Thomas Tilling Ltd who operated many of London's horsed buses. Horses were usually five years old when they started and served until they were 12.

Right: Kennington Fire Station, 1905

Horses were generally stabled at fire stations and were the responsibility of coachmen who would also reside at the station. The harnesses were suspended from the ceiling of the appliance room, and then dropped onto the horses' backs when required. The stations also had sloped exits to help horses pulling the heavy steam fire engines to gather momentum as they raced to a fire. This led to the introduction of the phrase 'on the run', a term still used by the Brigade today.

Date of Offence.	Name of Offence.	Where Stationed with name of Officer in charge.	Witnesses.	Award.	By wh award
June 21st 1884	Absent from the station without leave about 40 minutes Suspended.			Fined " 3 6	
Nov 5th 1884	Under the influence of drink & unfit for duty on his return from a fire at 11.35 pm Suspended.			Fined " 4 "	
May 15th 1889	Carelessly driving No. 16 Clerkenwell Fire Van and thereby knocking down & injuring a child.		Cautioned		
April 26th 1891	One hour & 7 minutes over leave.			Fined " 2 6	
April 24th 1891.	Breach of discipline in sending a letter to the Chairman of the Fire Brigade Committee.		Cautioned		
June 25th 1892	Carelessness in driving No. 12 Escape Van thereby causing the escape to collide with and damage the brickwork of the North East Archway at Head Quarters also breaking the near side of the main ladder of the escape		Cautioned		

Robert Stanley, coachman, c.1890

The duties of a coachman included caring for the horses and tacking up when a call was received. They were responsible for manoeuvering the appliance through the busy streets of London and on arrival they were required to lead the horses away from the incident. If necessary, they would take messages from the scene of the fire back to the station using one of the horses as transport.

Left: Robert Stanley, discipline section, 1887–1892

Extract from a coachman's service record describing Robert Stanley damaging a vehicle in a crash.

Right: Cannon Street Fire Station, c.1913

The conscription of horses during the First World War resulted in the rapid introduction of motorised appliances to outer London brigades. In London, motor cars were used first as senior officers' transport. Motor fire engines soon followed with Commer motor escape vans and Merryweather motor pumps. Fire stations were modified to accommodate these new vehicles. The stables were removed and appliance bay doors widened.

The last horses used by London Fire Brigade, November 1921
The horses, which always worked in pairs, were traditionally known as the 'Brigade Greys'. The last two horses, Nora and Lucy, were stationed at Kensington Fire Station and were used to pull the turntable ladder. They stopped service in 1921.

Architecture

Poplar Fire Station, 1870s
The architect for the Metropolitan Fire Brigade from 1866 until 1870 was Edward Cresy. His style was typically Victorian, with solid malm (a mixture of clay and chalk) bricks, relieved by red brick and Milton tiles.

London Fire Brigade Headquarters, Southwark, 1920s

In 1878, the new fire brigade headquarters building opened in Southwark Bridge Road. Designed and built by Hook and Oldrey, it cost £70,000. The new headquarters included areas for administration, workshops, a drill tower, a practise area and accommodation for firefighters and their families. The Chief Officer Captain Sir Eyre Massey Shaw lived, on site, in Winchester House.

Bishopsgate Fire Station, 1910

When the architect Alfred Mott took on the task of designing new fire stations he introduced a strong gothic style. By 1877, the Metropolitan Fire Brigade had 48 fire stations, 107 escape ladder stations and four river stations.

Camden Fire Station, 1907

In the 1880s many new fire stations were built. Overseen by the archtect Robert Pearsall, the new stations had a distinctive angular outline, with paired windows, careful detailing and crenulated look-out towers. They were often five or six storeys high, providing accommodation for firefighters and their families. Below, there were two or three bays for steam fire engines and escapes.

Cherry Garden River Station, *c.*1900

In 1894, there were proposals to build six new fire stations and over 100 substations. The substations included mobile station posts for escape ladders and watchmen. By 1898 London had 59 stations, five river stations, 16 street stations and 156 watch boxes. In 1904 the chairman of the London County Council reported a new fire station was being opened every two months.

Euston Fire Station, 1930s

The period of 1905 to 1921 saw the Brigade fleet fully motorised, and fire stations were altered to accomodate these new vehicles. Wider doors were needed to allow motor engines to exit fire stations easily. The accommodation for horses was removed or changed into workshops. Electricity was introduced, as well as telegraph systems. By the 1920s firefighters below the rank of station officer were allowed to live away from the fire station.

**London Fire Brigade Headquarters, Lambeth,
under construction, 1936**

1934 saw approval for a new fire brigade
headquarters building on the Albert Embankment.
It opened in 1937, and had an appliance bay for
seven fire engines. It was 10 storeys high and had
accommodation for officers as well as office staff.
There was a drill yard at the back of the building for
training, and a balcony with seating for 800 people
to watch the weekly displays by the Brigade.

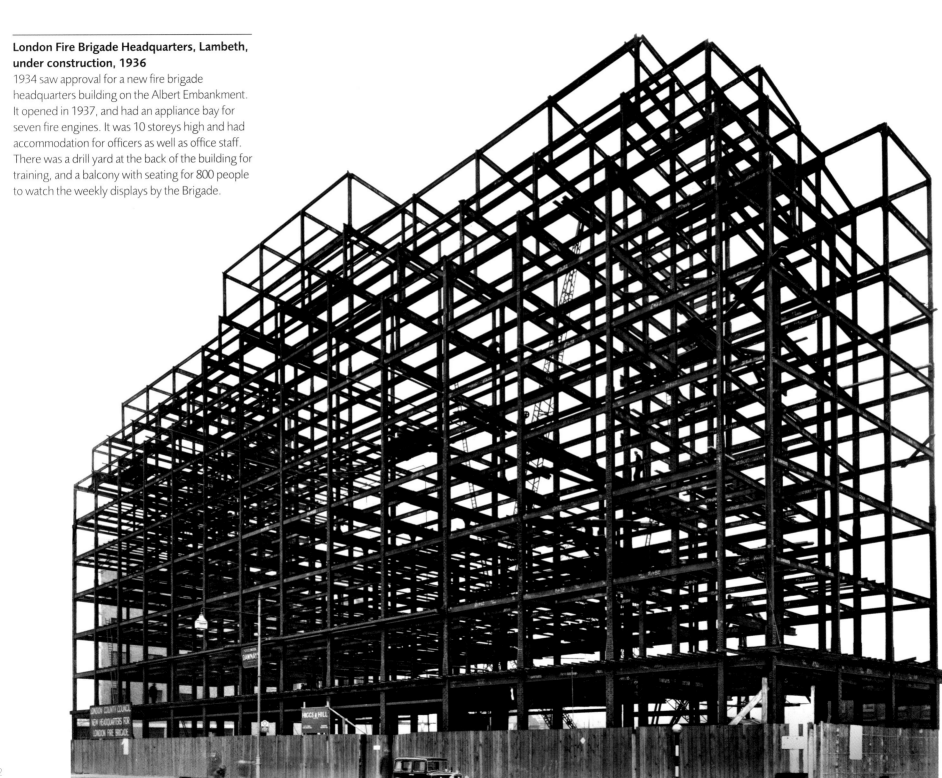

London Fire Brigade Headquarters, Lambeth, 1937
The new headquarters were opened by King George VI. In the main reception hall a permanent memorial was erected to those who had died on duty with London Fire Brigade.

Far left: Chelsea Fire Station, 1965

The Greater London Council, created in 1965, oversaw the building of stations across London, from Middlesex, Croydon and West Ham out into Kent, Essex and Surrey. They had a simpler, more efficient design than their Victorian predecessors. Under the GLC, the number of London fire stations grew to 124.

Left: Barnet Fire Station, 1991

In 1986, a new command structure prompted the refurbishment of fire stations that acted as area headquarters. Throughout the 1990s, fewer new fire stations were built in favour of making improvements to existing stations.

Left: Mitcham Fire Station, 2015

To meet the needs of a 21st century fire and rescue service, a station rebuilding programme is a key part of the Brigade's commitment to providing a flexible, efficient and effective fire and rescue service for London. The new fire stations will replace buildings that are in a poor condition and no longer meet modern requirements. The project will result in nine new fire stations, which will see some of the capital's oldest fire stations replaced and updated.

Recruitment and training

"It is a quiet morning and in the quadrangle recruits are being drilled...
in the instruction room they have been shown sections of valves and
boilers, and taught the theory of them; now a group are swarming over
a real, live engine, and learning all about her. Not far away a new escape
is being tested from top to bottom by half a dozen men, who attach
ropes, mount the wheels and spring off in a body, so as to put a sudden
and heavy strain on each part. Keen and severe is the testing system."

Extract from *London's Fire Brigade* by Walter P. Wright, *c.*1900

Above: Metropolitan Fire Brigade recruitment strength test, *c.* 1898
The first Chief Officer of the Metropolitan Fire Brigade (MFB) Captain Sir Eyre Massey Shaw favoured recruitment of men from the navy. He felt that the trainees would be disciplined and would require less training, making the recruitment process more efficient. Recruitment tests for the MFB included the lifting of a weight of 244lbs (150 kilos), and the completion of a dictation exercise.

Right: Reference for Walter J. Osborne, 1912
Recruits were also expected to provide character references, and measure no less than 37 inches around the chest and being at least 5 ft 5 ins in height.

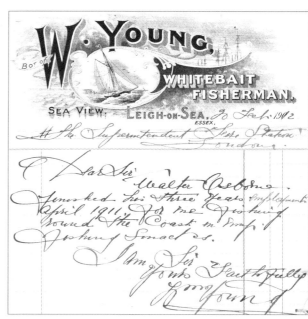

Far left: Rescue drills at Southwark Training Centre, 1920s

Training to be an MFB firefighter lasted for two months and then firefighters were on probation for a further three months at a fire station. From 1878 drill class took place at Southwark Training Centre. The site was also home to Captain Sir Eyre Massey Shaw who fitted balconies to the building, to enable him to watch firefighters throughout their training.

Left: Jump sheet drill at Southwark Training Centre, 1931

Training included learning how to operate a fire engine, ladder drills, first aid and the use of jump sheets and chair knots to rescue people from a height. A jump sheet had to be held taut by a minimum of 14 men in order to catch the escaping person without causing injury.

Above: Firefighters receiving knot instructions at Southwark Training Centre, 1933

After Captain Sir Eyre Massey's retirement in 1891 it was no longer compulsory for recruits to have naval experience. However recruitment from the navy was preferred until the Second World War. Many of the phrases used by the Brigade today have a naval influence with ropes being referred to as lines and a watch system used for shift patterns.

Above and left: National Fire Service firefighters at an assault course training camp, 1943

As a prelude to the Second World War, fire service recruitment in London began in March 1938. There were queues of people outside fire stations, eager to join. On 1 September 1939 about 89,000 men and 6,000 women were mobilised countrywide for full-time service in the Auxiliary Fire Service, and war was declared two days later on 3 September 1939.

Wartime training was initially for 60 hours in total, and included drilling and practising with equipment. Firefighters' training differed throughout the country and it was not until the formation of the National Fire Service in 1941 that a drill book was issued to standardise training methods.

Right: Lord Mayor's Show, 1949

The Cold War period, after the Second World War, led to the re-formation of the Auxiliary Fire Service in 1948. Once again men and women were recruited into the wholly voluntary service. After the war, large events such as the Lord Mayor's Show were used to encourage people to sign up.

Left: Post-war Auxiliary Fire Service recruitment drive, 1953
The government aimed to have one auxiliary firefighter for every whole-time firefighter, in case of a large scale incident or nuclear attack. The post war Auxiliary Fire Service was disbanded in 1968.

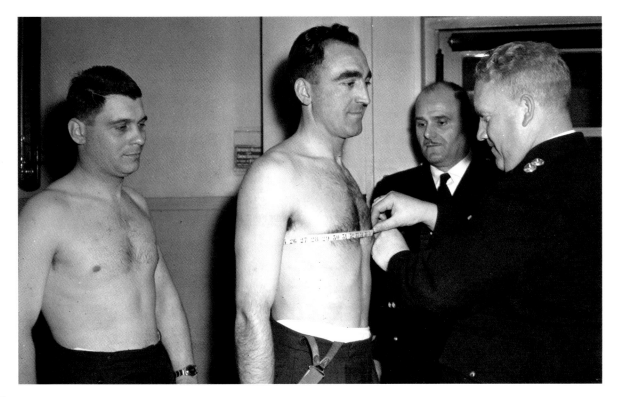

Left: Chest measurement of a London Fire Brigade applicant, 1950s – 1960s
A candidate for London Fire Brigade during this period had to be aged between 19 and 30, and firefighters had to be at least 5 ft 7 ins in height. A chest measurement of not less than 36 inches was required with a minimum expansion of two inches. Recruits also had to have good sight and hearing, as well as good teeth.

Right: Trainee firefighters at Lambeth headquarters, 1959
After the war, training for firefighters lasted for nine weeks and included drills and a morning and evening parade. Initial training did not include courses in breathing apparatus, instead firefighters returned a year later, after their probationary period, to complete a two-week programme. From 1937 until the 1960s all training was at Lambeth headquarters rather than Southwark Training Centre.

Above: Junior firemen learning to drive, 1966

With a shortage of recruits in the 1960s, a junior firemen scheme was established for boys aged between 16 and 17. Junior firemen were not only given training in firefighting but were taught to drive and swim, and attended 'outward bound' training courses.

Top right: Southwark Training Centre group passing out photograph, 1986

With the formation of the Greater London Council, London Fire Brigade's responsibility grew to cover more than 32 London boroughs, incorporating many outer London brigades. Training continued at Southwark Training Centre with additional facilities being used at Finchley. Upon completion of training, firefighters attended a passing out ceremony as a final exam. It was not until the late 1970s that this became a ceremonial family event and sometimes featured a demonstration of the skills learnt by the newly qualified firefighters.

Right: Park Royal Training Centre, 2015

Firefighter training currently takes place at two new training facilities at Park Royal and Beckton. The Park Royal venue features a four storey zero-emission fire house which allows firefighters to carry out fire and breathing apparatus training in a range of challenging real fire scenarios. This includes simulating fires in houses and commercial buildings and basements. The centre, which covers 4,000 square metres, and runs around 500 training courses a year, also provides a tower for ladder and line rescue training, as well as classroom facilities.

The workforce

Left: London Fire Brigade photographers making a cine-film recording, *c*.1936
Throughout its 150 year history, the Brigade has kept a photographic record of fires and emergencies. Over the years, thousands of photographs and hours of film have been recorded to document incidents and capture vital moments of the Brigade's history.

Above: National Fire Service women, *c*.1942
The outbreak of the Second World War in 1939 was the first time that women were able to join the fire service.

Their responsibilities included driving mobile canteen vans, to ensure firefighters had vital food and drink supplies whilst tackling huge blazes, which sometimes lasted for days and nights on end.

In addition to their driving duties, some women were required to service and maintain the vehicles that they drove.

Right: Auxiliary Fire Service female dispatch riders, *c*.1940
Women volunteered at their local fire station for jobs involving communications, dispatching messages and driving vehicles. Women often had to navigate vehicles during times of blackout, through dark roads without sign posts.

Above left: Hose workshop, Lambeth headquarters, c.1953
Firefighters were supported by a vast array of staff employed in a variety of key roles. This included the highly skilled mechanics, carpenters and expert craftsmen.

Above right: Vehicle repair workshop, Lambeth headquarters, c.1953
The principal repair workshop was situated behind the headquarters building at Lambeth. Within this workshop complex, fire engines were repaired and serviced, ladders were built, couplings were wired onto hose lengths, and radio equipment was maintained.

Right: Fire Brigades Union Contribution Card, 1948
The earliest evidence of trade union activity in London can be traced back to 1906. It was not until 1918, however, that the Fire Brigades Union (FBU) was formed and duly recognised, which was closely linked to the ending of the First World War. The FBU has gone on to play a significant role in LFB's history, working closely with firefighters and fire and rescue services across the UK.

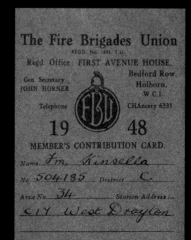

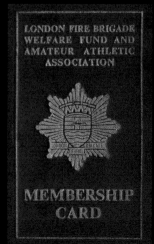

Below: London Fire Brigade control room, c.1987
Similar to firefighters, control room staff work all year round in a watch shift system, including public holidays. Control staff take emergency 999 calls, find out details of incidents and deploy Brigade resources to emergencies.

Left: Welfare Fund Membership Card, c.1950
The LFB Welfare Society was set up to encourage sporting, recreational and social activities to London Fire Brigade staff. The Welfare Fund, as it is now known, continues to run competitions, events and trips abroad for its members. Firefighters and other staff have also been supported over the years by the Benevolent Fund, a national organisation now known as The Fire Fighters Charity.

Right: Sue Batten, 1982
Following a major recruitment campaign by the Greater London Council, Sue Batten joined London Fire Brigade as the first UK female firefighter in 1982. Around 60 other women joined in the 1980s. There are now more than 300 women firefighters working for London Fire Brigade.

London firefighters wearing the new work wear uniform, 2014

London Fire Brigade strives to represent the vibrant and diverse community it serves through its workforce. To ensure this, there are a number of measures in place, including targeted recruitment and career development, support groups, equality and diversity training for all staff and equality impact assessments.

Queen Elizabeth II opening the new headquarters and meeting non-operational staff, 2007

London's fire and rescue service is the busiest in the country and one of the largest in the world. Frontline services are supported by non-operational, non-uniformed staff whose roles include community fire safety, education, IT, human resources and procurement.

Celebrations and commemorations

Presentation of long service medals, Southwark headquarters, 1915
The first medals issued by the Metropolitan Fire Brigade were in 1877 and were presented to firefighters for acts of bravery. Since that date medals have been presented to Brigade staff for gallantry and long service, and to commemorate royal occasions. Long service medals are awarded to all members of local authority fire brigades, whether full or part-time, for a minimum of 20 years' exemplary service.

Section Officer Pennington with OBE medal, 1941
The bravery of members of the fire service in London during the Second World War was recognised with the awarding of one George Cross, 38 George Medals, one CBE, three OBEs, 13 MBEs and 118 BEMs.

Two London firefighters celebrating their George Medal awards, 1941

During the Second World War there were many acts of bravery by firefighters. Gillian Tanner was the only female firefighter to be awarded the George Medal for her bravery during the war. On 29 December 1940, a particularly severe night in the Blitz, she drove around London's flaming streets in a lorry loaded with petrol, in order to fill up trailer pumps.

The only George Cross medal to be awarded to a London firefighter during the war was that given to Harry Errington. Errington's fire station on Rathbone Street received a direct hit, and despite suffering from severe burns he rescued three of his fellow firefighters.

Firefighters give three cheers for the annual review's Inspecting Officer, Lord Snell of Plumstead, Chairman of the London County Council, 1925

Annual reviews were often held at venues across London including Clapham Common, Hyde Park, Victoria Park and the Brigade's headquarters. The reviews provided the opportunity to highlight the skill and reputation of the Brigade. Medals were awarded to firefighters and important figures including King George V, the Prince of Wales and the Chairman of the London County Council made inspections. By the 1960s the reviews had almost become a national event as there was such a high demand for tickets.

London Fire Brigade headquarters, opening ceremony, 1937

The Brigade's headquarters site in Lambeth was officially opened on 21 July 1937 by King George VI and 150 firefighters paraded for Royal inspection. The headquarters held displays every Wednesday for members of the public, who had to apply in writing for tickets from the Chief Officer.

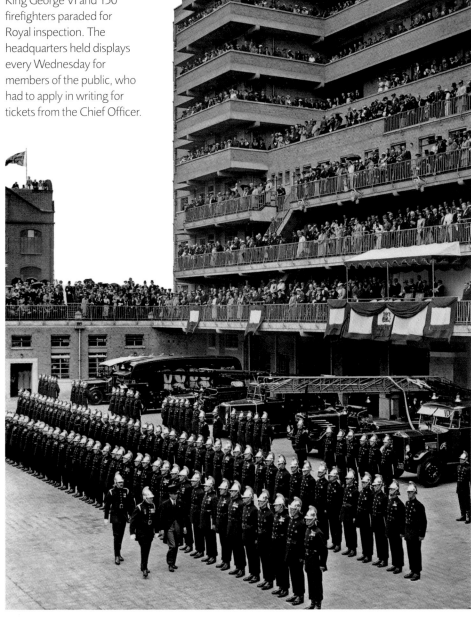

Centenary celebrations of London Fire Brigade, Lambeth, 1966

The year 1966 marked the centenary of London Fire Brigade and the 300th anniversary of the outbreak of the Great Fire of London. As part of the celebrations, the Brigade organised a River Pageant at Lambeth and a commemorative display, which was attended by Queen Elizabeth II and the Duke of Edinburgh.

Above left: London Fire Brigade tug of war team, 1923

A Brigade sports day became an annual occasion from the beginning of the 20th century, with the Chief Officer regularly attending. Sports days included events such as boxing, cycling, cricket and football. More unusual events such as tilting the bucket and a wandering bandsmen race also featured.

Above right: Alfie Shawyer, boxing champion, c.1938

Alfie Shawyer, who became Assistant Chief Officer, was a prominent figure in boxing during the 1930s and 40s. He became the British Amateur Champion and won the prestigious Golden Gloves of America.

Opposite, top right: London Fire Brigade band at Lambeth headquarters, 1939

The Brigade band was formed in the 1920s and was initially sponsored by Lloyds of London in gratitude for the wartime courage of London Fire Brigade. All of the members were firefighters, but many had never played an instrument before. The Guildhall School of Music provided instruction and weekly concerts were held at Lambeth headquarters, with an annual performance at the Queen's Hall.

Opposite, bottom right: London Fire Brigade firefighters in the 100-yard race, White City Stadium, 1958

The London Fire Brigade Athletic Association was founded in 1889. The Association aimed to encourage staff to compete, to help develop future champions, with firefighters and their families alike able to attend and participate. In 1968 Firefighter Ian Alsop competed in the Olympic Games in Mexico.

Left: London Fire Brigade firefighters in a whaler race, River Thames, 1958

Whaler racing was popular in London Fire Brigade, with a team competing annually against crews from the Thames Division of the Metropolitan Police and the Royal Naval Volunteer Reserve. The winners received a cup presented by the Worshipful Company of Fishmongers.

Above: UK Rescue Challenge, London Fire Brigade line rescue team, ExCel London, 2011

Right: LFB running vest for staff participating in the London Marathon, 2015

After 150 years trainee fitness is still paramount and firefighters continue to excel in competitive events including the London Marathon, Three Peaks Challenge, United Kingdom Rescue Challenge and World Rescue Challenge.

Fire engines and vehicles

Left: Shand Mason six-inch manual pump, c.1870

In use from the 1840s, these large manual pumps were a later example of those designed by Richard Newsham in the early 1700s. The stretcher handles on each side allowed teams of twenty people to pump up to 150 gallons per minute, although it was only possible for someone to pump continuously for five minutes before becoming exhausted. These pumps carried scaling ladders and leather delivery hose. Driven by a coachman, this horse-drawn pump could only carry four firefighters to the fire.

Right: Horsed escape van, c.1900

Wheeled escape ladders were first introduced by the Royal Society for the Protection of Life from Fire in 1836. They were positioned on street corners and were operated by an escape conductor. The MFB took over street escape stations in 1866 and the first horse-drawn escapes were introduced in the 1890s. They only carried a 50ft (15.24m) wheeled escape ladder and rescue lines, however later versions featured first aid tanks and hose reel.

Right: Shand Mason steam fire engine, c.1890

Steam fire engines were invented in 1829 by Braithwaite and Ericsson, however it was not until the 1860s that a variety of steam engines were being manufactured en masse. The Chief Officer of the Metropolitan Fire Brigade (MFB) declared that each fire station should have at least one steam engine. They were more powerful and economical than the manual pumps, pumping up to 350 gallons a minute. This extra capacity was needed to combat the growing number of fires in the increasingly industrialised city.

Left: Merryweather Fire King, self-propelled steam engine, 1900s

The Fire King was introduced in London in 1905. The steam engine was used to power the pump as well as the rear wheels which propelled the fire engine at a low speed, removing the need for horses. It was paraffin fired and could pump for two hours on full power. Although these appliances remained in use until 1912, their excessive weight reduced turnout times and they struggled on slopes and inclines.

Right: Merryweather Hatfield motor pump, c.1909

The Hatfield motor pump proved to be a very reliable vehicle. Following its introduction, the Brigade committed to expanding the motorised fleet. From 1912 and into the 1920s Dennis N-Types with centrifugal pumps were allocated to almost every station. This was a marked improvement on the use of cylinders in the earlier Hatfield pumps, which had a poor power-to-weight ratio and were significantly larger than the compact centrifugal pumps.

Dennis emergency tender, c.1913

The first emergency tender was designed to provide additional equipment at serious incidents, including breathing apparatus, heavy lifting equipment and flood lighting via a generator which could be operated on or off the vehicle. It was not compulsory for firefighters to be trained in the use of breathing apparatus, therefore emergency tenders required a fully trained specialist crew.

Dennis Magirus turntable ladder, *c.*1925
Magirus turntable ladders were manufactured in Germany and
were originally made from wood. Their maximum height was
85ft (25.9m). Early versions of these ladders were horse drawn,
but towards the end of the First World War, many of these
ladders were transferred to motor-driven or electric chassis.

Above: Dennis Lancet hose-laying lorry, *c*.1936
This was the first high speed hose-laying lorry to be commissioned by London Fire Brigade. It was brought into service in 1937 and could carry two miles of large diameter hose. It was the forerunner of the many hose-laying lorries used by the water units during the Second World War and it remained in service until 1963. Modern hose-laying lorries are capable of laying hose at speeds of over 20mph and can retrieve the hose once it has been used.

Top right: Leyland Limousine dual purpose pump, *c*.1938
This fire engine was designed to be streamlined and ultra modern, setting the style for subsequent enclosed models. The first ever diesel fire engine was part of this fleet. Their ability to carry breathing apparatus inside the cab made them easier to use and they were later referred to as 'breathing apparatus pumps'.

Right: Dennis No.2 trailer pump and London taxi towing vehicle, *c*.1939
Trailer pumps were issued by the government during the Second World War for use by the Auxiliary Fire Service and subsequently the National Fire Service. Because of a shortage of suitable towing vehicles, LFB commandeered into service approximately two thousand London taxis, which were converted in the Brigade workshops to include tow bars and ladder racks.

Left: Bedford heavy unit with a Sulzer pump, c.1940

Heavy units were issued to assist the lighter trailer pumps used by the Auxiliary Fire Service. Most substations had at least one heavy pumping unit. The Sulzer pump was powered by a Ford V8 engine and had a pumping capacity of approximately 600 gallons a minute.

Bottom left: Leyland control unit, c.1952

Control units are used as forward command posts at major fires and incidents. They provide a radio link to Brigade control and act as a focal point for liaison between senior officers and other emergency services. The red and white chequered markings on the roof-mounted dome signify the role of the vehicle as a command post. Modern Command Support Units attend incidents with more than four crews in attendance and feature the latest communications technology.

Below: AEC Merryweather Regent dual purpose appliance, 1962

This diesel powered appliance was dual purpose, meaning that it could be used either as a pump or as a pump escape. A large part of the Brigade fleet consisted of this type of vehicle throughout the 1950s and 60s. It was capable of pumping 1,000 gallons a minute.

Top far left: Dennis F101 pump, *c.*1965

A fire appliance unique to London Fire Brigade, the F101 was a diesel powered dual purpose appliance, many of which were commissioned. Pump escapes superseded the motor escape vans of the pre-Second World War period, as many of these did not carry pumps.

Top left: Dennis Pax foam tender, *c.*1965

Introduced in the 1920s, foam tenders were designed to combat fires in volatile liquids such as oil, by blanketing the fire. They carried foam compound in an integral tank, which when mixed with water, provided large quantities of foam. Modern foam tenders carry containers of foam compound and foam generators. The chemical makeup of foam compound has improved significantly over the years.

Bottom far left: Dennis F108 pump, *c.*1970

A large number of these vehicles were brought into service in the 1970s until almost every London station housed an F108. They could be used as a pump or a pump escape and they featured a large 300 gallon water tank instead of the 100 gallon tanks of earlier vehicles.

Bottom left: Volvo FL6 Saxon pump ladder, 1997

This vehicle could store a range of rescue tools and apparatus in addition to its normal firefighting equipment. This was a standard appliance and all stations within the Brigade were issued with at least one. It carried a 13.5m ladder which was a replacement for the earlier wheeled escapes.

Simon Snorkel, Mercedes ALP, *c.*2006

Modern height vehicles have significantly progressed from the early, mechanically operated horse-drawn turntable ladders. The hydraulically operated aerial ladder platforms of today can reach heights of over 32m and have an articulating arm that can navigate obstacles, providing a secure location from which a firefighter can operate.

Mercedes-Benz Atego dual purpose ladder, in current use
This fire engine is the standard pump of London Fire Brigade. It carries hose, generators, airbags, breathing apparatus, floodlights, chemical protection suits and medical equipment. At stations with two pumps, one carries a 13.5m ladder and the other a 9m ladder. At stations with one pump, both ladders are carried on the same vehicle. These fire engines hold over 1,300 litres of water and can pump almost 4,000 litres a minute.

Mini Countryman, initial response vehicle, *c.*2012
These modified Mini Countrymans were designed specifically for use in the Olympic Park in Stratford. They provided an initial response to any small incidents that the Brigade attended during the London 2012 Olympic and Paralympic Games. The Minis were equipped to respond to small fires that did not require breathing apparatus and make routine patrols. The Minis continue to be used for community safety and other special events.

Fire boats

Above left: Fire boat Alpha II, *c.*1912
In 1900 a new self-propelled fire-float was brought into service by the Metropolitan Fire Brigade. The Alpha (later renamed the Alpha II) had a shallow draft and the first large deck-mounted monitor capable of delivering an enormous jet of water.

Above right: Fire boat Beta II, *c.*1910s
The Alpha II was later joined by an even more powerful vessel, the Beta II in 1906. The crews of these boats became known as 'floaties', a name which has continued to be used into modern times.

Left: Fire float and tug, *c.*1890
In 1893, the Brigade had a fleet of eight tug-and-barge combinations based at four river fire stations, at Pimlico, Charing Cross Pier, Shadwell Fish Market and Cherry Garden Pier. The floating barge carried the fire pump and was towed to incidents by a steam tug. This was a marked improvement on the earlier self-propelled boats, which had such a large draft they were unable to reach the shallow areas by the banks of the river.

Left: Massey Shaw fire boat, *c.*1930s
One of the best-known fire boats in the world, the Massey Shaw came into service in 1935. Designed with a very shallow draft, she was ideal for the tidal waters of the Thames. With an incredibly high pumping capacity of 3,000 gallons per minute at 100psi, she could deliver up to 75 tons of water a minute, enough to punch a hole through a warehouse wall.

Above left: Massey Shaw fire boat returning from Dunkirk, *c.*1940
The Massey Shaw fire boat's most famous exploit came in May 1940, when the British Expeditionary Force, together with French and Belgian forces, was trapped on the beaches surrounding Dunkirk. A major operation was initiated to evacuate these troops, known as 'Operation Dynamo'. London Fire Brigade was approached for assistance and the Massey Shaw fire boat was dispatched to France to assist in the evacuation. She made several trips and rescued hundreds of soldiers. On her return across the Channel she also rescued many sailors and soldiers from a sinking French warship. Once back in London, Massey Shaw and her crew received a hero's welcome before being plunged into the Blitz.

Above right: London Region National Fire Service fire floats and tenders, *c.*1941
During the Second World War, the number of river fire stations was increased to 18. In preparation for the war a major fire boat, the James Braidwood, was added to the regular fleet and an additional ten smaller fire boats, called the Thames Class, were ordered. These boats were used by the Auxiliary Fire Service and were distributed to the existing and new floating stations. After the start of the war another 10 Thames boats were ordered and other suitable vessels were converted to operate as fire boats. These included narrowboats, which could access canals and carry trailer pumps, to supply vital water during bombing raids.

Left: London Phoenix fire boat, 1985

Smaller, faster fire boats followed the Massey Shaw and James Braidwood into service throughout the 1960s and 1970s, including the Fire Swift and Fire Hawk. They were followed in March 1985 by what may have been the world's first catamaran fire boat, the London Phoenix. The Phoenix initially had a hydraulic platform but this proved to be unstable and it was later removed. It was equipped for both conventional firefighting and oil fires, with a substantial foam-making capacity.

Below: The Fire Dart on the River Thames, *c.* 2004

The Fireflash and Firedart are ultra modern vessels that combine the role of a fire boat with that of a fast rescue craft, they came into operation in 1999. Their speed enables them to conduct rapid water rescues and they are designed to take on and deploy crews easily and quickly. One of the boats is permanently crewed at all times, while the other craft is kept in reserve. Both vessels are based at the Brigade's floating fire station at Lambeth.

Uniforms

"One fireman from Cannon Street Station remembers getting a fire call one evening when, training for a boxing tournament, he was wearing black athletic tights. Slipping into his fire boots and waterproof leggings, he sailed out on his appliance to find that, having no trousers on, there was nothing to keep his leggings up. It was night and there was nothing for it but to discard his leggings and trust that the darkness would prevent his being reported for 'being improperly dressed at a fire.' He got away with it; but he was very cold."

Extract from *Fire Service Memories*
by Commander Sir Aylmer Firebrace, 1949

Presentation of gallantry medals, *c.*1936
The brass helmet was in use from the 1860s until 1936,
the longest serving helmet in Brigade history. The first
Chief Officer of the Brigade, Captain Sir Eyre Massey
Shaw was inspired by the French *Pompiers* he saw in
Paris. He designed the helmet to be lightweight, well
ventilated and constructed in sections so that it could
easily be repaired. Captain Shaw himself wore a
distinctive sliver-coated helmet. This has influenced
the yellow and white helmets since worn by firefighters
and officers respectively. The distinctive dragon emblem
that decorates the central comb is believed to have
been designed by Shaw's daughter Anna.

Left: Firefighter Soggee, *c*.1900
The double-breasted navy blue serge tunic, a mainstay of Brigade fire gear, was warm, practical and smart. Woollen trousers, leather boots and a leather belt completed the uniform.

Right: Firefighters from Knightsbridge Fire Station, 1912
Firefighters, when not fighting fires, wore a round cap similar to those worn by sailors, reflecting the Brigade's policy of recruiting only ex-seamen.

Far right: London Fire Brigade firefighter, *c*.1937
Black waterproof leggings were introduced in about 1900 to prevent trousers becoming waterlogged and heavy. As the use of electricity became more widespread, a compressed cork helmet was introduced in 1936. It was covered in linen and could withstand up to 11,000 volts. It featured a gold-painted high comb that protected firefighters from falling debris. But this headwear was in use only until 1939, owing to the onset of the Second World War.

Right: National Fire Service firefighter, 1941
During the Second World War, the cork helmet was replaced by a military style steel helmet designed to protect firefighters from rubble and shrapnel. The matt khaki colour helped to camouflage them from enemy bombers, whilst the waxed cotton 'curtain' flap at the back protected their necks.

Middle: Firefighters using a railing expander to release a trapped boy, c.1950
Following the Second World War, the Brigade returned to using cork helmets. The new helmets were painted black, with a solid cork comb and a high gloss finish.

Opposite: London Fire Brigade annual review and inspection at Lambeth headquarters, 1955
Number 1 dress uniform was designed to be worn at parades and official events. The uniform featured a peaked cap.

Far left: Firefighters at the King's Cross underground fire, 1987
In 1972, the Uniform Committee of the Central Fire Brigades Advisory Council recommended that firefighters' helmets be painted canary yellow, to increase their visibility. Yellow over-trousers were introduced to make firefighters even more noticeable.

Left: Firefighters at an eight pump fire on Fenchurch Street, 1991
In 1989 the yellow cork helmet was replaced by the Pacific helmet. This was constructed from lightweight Kevlar and fibreglass without the traditional high comb. London was one of the first brigades in the UK to introduce a helmet with the added protection of a tough transparent visor. The blue serge tunic, which had been in use since the 1860s was replaced by the Nomex uniform. Nomex was engineered to be heatproof, flame resistant and waterproof.

Above: Firefighters extinguishing a fire at Staples Corner, c.2005
The Cromwell F600 helmet was introduced in 1999. Made from tough heatproof fibreglass it featured a full protective visor and, like the Victorian brass helmet, was made in several parts, allowing component pieces to be easily replaced if broken. The new maroon red Inferno uniform featured improved high visibility strips.

Firefighters wearing new personal protective equipment, 2010
In 2010, the Brigade introduced the Gallet F1 helmet, made from injected thermoplastic and featuring an integral face shield and safety glasses. State of the art Personal Protective Equipment (PPE) consisting of a fire hood, tunic, leggings, gloves and boots completed the new uniform.

Breathing apparatus

Smoke Helmet

Far left: Demonstration of a smoke helmet, *c*.1900s

Introduced in the early 1900s, Siebe Gorman smoke helmets were the first real attempt to provide a fresh air supply to firefighters working in dense smoke. Air entered the helmet through breathing tubes connected to a set of bellows at each side, operated by a second person. The firefighter wearing the helmet could communicate with the bellows operator by strategic tugs on a line, if he wanted more or less air, or if he got into trouble. The problem with this breathing apparatus (BA) was that the firefighters' movements were restricted to the length of the hose.

Left: Crew of Emergency Tender wearing early Proto breathing apparatus, Clerkenwell, *c*.1914

The first type of self-contained breathing apparatus was the Salvus set, designed in Germany and originally used in mines. The Salvus set was quickly replaced by a more streamlined version called the Proto set. The Mark 1 Proto set consisted of a cylinder of oxygen and an air reservoir or breathing bag containing an absorbent, which removed the carbon dioxide; it was then mixed with a fresh supply of oxygen and reused.

Below: Firefighters wearing Proto breathing apparatus, *c*. late 1920s

Firefighters emerging from a warehouse fire in the 1930s wearing Mark 1 Proto breathing apparatus sets.

Left: Emergency Tender crew wearing Mark 4 Proto breathing apparatus, c.1938

Breathing apparatus sets were carried on a few designated pumps and also on the Brigade's two emergency tenders.

Top right: Auxiliary Fire Service breathing apparatus training using Proto sets, 1943

Proto BA sets continued to be modified and improved over the years, and firefighters had a strict training and maintenance programme to ensure that the sets always worked efficiently at all times. Later models of the Proto set were fitted with full face masks as an alternative to the mouthpiece, goggles and nose clips.

Below right: Firefighter in training, 2001

This type of compressed air BA set is designed on an open circuit system where exhaled air is discharged to the atmosphere and not purified for reuse as it had been in the earlier oxygen sets. It featured a cylinder containing pressurised air, a respiratory system supplying the wearer with air on demand according to their needs and a face mask.

Far right: Breathing apparatus control board, 2011

Following the fatal fire at Smithfield Meat Market in 1958, it was recommended that a formal method of controlling breathing apparatus at incidents be developed. The BA control board was introduced shortly afterwards, featuring coloured tags representing the type of BA set, the name of the firefighter, the amount of oxygen in the set, on entry into a fire and the time that they entered. This allowed the BA controller to monitor each member of the crew at the scene of an emergency.

BA control boards have developed significantly, and newer designs feature a live telemetry system allowing the controller to see how much air the wearer has left and how much longer they can remain in the incident. Evacuation signals can also be sent to the control board in the event of an emergency.

Firefighters wearing duration Dräger breathing apparatus, 2011

Modern standard duration BA sets feature a fully adjustable harness and carrying system as well as vastly improved connections for quicker service and maintainance. Cylinders can hold up to 2,000 litres of air, lasting more than 30 minutes. Sets are fitted with monitoring devices which alert the wearer when the cylinder pressure drops to a predetermined level. BA teams consist of a miminum of two firefighters, to ensure their safety when entering a smoke-filled building.

Communications

Left: Firefighters in a control room, 1902

To enable communications between fire stations the Metropolitan Fire Brigade used the highly efficient Siemen and Halskes' electric telegraph system.

Right: London Fire Brigade street fire alarm and telephone point, *c.*1930s

Prior to 1880 the only way to notify the Brigade of a fire was to use a running call, with a messenger relaying information to a fire station. After this date, street fire alarms were installed. For maximum visibility they were positioned on pavements at street corners. These alarms were in direct contact, by landline, with the local fire station. When activated manually by the caller the alarm bell sounded in the fire station, indicating the location of the alarm.

Far right: Children examine a street telephone fire alarm in the 1940s

The use of street fire alarms contributed to a rise in hoax calls, as the alarms were often set off unnecessarily. This became such a concern that in 1895 an Act of Parliament prohibited false alarms, with a maximum penalty of a £25 fine or three months' imprisonment. These fire alarms were taken out of use in 1958 as the vast increase in the number of home and phone box telephones rendered them obsolete.

Left: London Fire Brigade control room, Lambeth headquarters, c.1940s

In 1948 a new control room was opened at London Fire Brigade headquarters in Lambeth, where all 999 calls were received. Many people were reluctant to embrace the change, amid concerns that the public telephone boxes might not always be in working order. It was also seen as a slower system, with calls going to an exchange rather than directly to a fire station. However with one central control room all fire engines could be mobilised from one location making operations much easier to coordinate.

Above left: London Fire Brigade motorcycle dispatch riders in training, c.1940

The Auxiliary Fire Service recruited messengers with the responsibility of relaying messages to different crews of firefighters during periods when control centres were unable to operate. Boys as young as 16 could enrol as long as they owned a bike. In addition, dispatch riders used motorcycles to drive through smoke and rubble to relay messages back to local fire control rooms.

Above: A woman dialling 999, c.1957

The first public phone box appeared in 1905. Gradually telephones replaced the telegraph for general communications within the Brigade, and the Post Office organised the new 999 system, agreeing to replace fire alarm posts with telephone boxes. People could call for the fire, police or ambulance services free of charge.

London Fire Brigade control room, Lambeth headquarters, 1998
The Brigade's Command and Mobilising Centre was opened in 1990 and by 1997 had received over two million calls. Emergency calls to the Brigade were no longer primarily fire-related but also included road and rail crashes, trapped members of the public and incidents involving spillages of hazardous materials.

London Operation Centre, control room, Merton, 2013
Control officers use an Integrated Communication Control System. This allows officers to receive and manage 999 calls as well as radio traffic. Geographical mobilising has also been introduced, enabling control to know the exact location of fire engines to improve attendance times. Advanced information will also be supplied from 999 calls to track where calls are being made from, to help determine the location of a fire.

Turning points

"It was weird ... nothing but fire and smoke to be seen everywhere; telegraph poles bursting into flames for no apparent reason and now the bloody road starts heaving."
Wartime firefighter, 1940–41

Theatre fires

Fire at the Theatre Royal, Drury Lane, 1908

During the Victorian period theatres were a high fire risk because of the gas lamps lighting the stage and the flammable materials used in the construction of the sets, combined with limited means of escape for audiences. The Chief Officer of the Metropolitan Fire Brigade wrote extensively about overcoming these risks. This led to an introduction of safety regulations for theatres including the use of fire safety curtains to separate the stage and the audience, to reduce the spread of the fire.

Warehouse fires

Above and overleaf: Warehouse fire, Butler's Wharf, Bermondsey, 1931

In the Victorian era the buildings along the docks were exempt from the buildings regulation act. Warehouses were often huge and storage rooms were undivided. The fire at Butler's Wharf broke out on a bitterly cold day on 9 March 1931. It was so cold that icicles formed on the ladders and the spray from the fireboats froze while tackling the blaze.

Warehouse fires

Above: Fireboat tackling a fire at Colonial Wharf, East London, 1935

At Colonial Wharf, a five storey warehouse burnt for four days and 600 firefighters attended the incident with 60 fire engines and three fireboats. This was one of the earliest tests for the Massey Shaw fireboat. She helped to prevent the fire from spreading to the surrounding buildings.

Right: Warehouse fire, Langley Street, 1954

This warehouse fire occurred in Covent Garden with fatal consequences, three firefighters died as the building collapsed.

Far right: Fire at a large records storage warehouse, Bow, 2006

The materials contained in many warehouses, and their vast size, ensures that they still remain a huge fire risk.

The First World War

Above: Southgate Fire Brigade, outer London brigade ready to assist under DORA, *c.*1914

The First World War impacted on London Fire Brigade, due to the Defence of the Realm Act (DORA) being passed in 1914. This gave the Chief Officer the authority to organise control of outer London brigades for assistance in case of air raids or attack. In addition many firefighters were called up as they were army or navy reservists. To support the reduced numbers, organisations such as the London Rifle Volunteers, the Salvage Corps and works brigades volunteered their services. Raids during this period were often random, and many incendiary bombs were ineffective. However, on 13 June 1917 a major attack on London, resulting in the death of a firefighter, led the government to recall surviving London Fire Brigade reservists from the front line.

The Second World War

Right: Auxiliary Fire Service firefighters taking refreshments at a fire, *c.*1940

During the Phoney War (a relatively quiet period on the homefront, before the Blitz began) the expected air raids did not occur and firefighters were thought of as 'army dodgers'. The beginning of the Blitz brought an end to this.

Left: A direct hit on sub-fire station 86W, located at Cavendish Road School, Balham, 5 November 1940

On 7 September 1940, with the start of the Blitz, the attitude towards firefighters changed dramatically. Many sacrificed their lives to protect London and became known as 'the heroes with grimy faces'.

Far left: Oxford Street after an air raid, 1940

Bombing raids, during the Blitz mostly occured at night and firefighters spent long hours putting out fires. Their work would often continue into the next morning.

Below left: Fire engines caught in the Blitz, 1940s

In order to support the fire service during the war additional fire engines were introduced. The most common was the trailer pump, for which the Brigade hired over 2,000 taxis as towing vehicles. Trailer pumps could be used to relay water, often from the river or an emergency water supply, to areas where it was needed. However during many of the worst air raids firefighters had to control fires with limited amounts of water.

Right: Corner store ablaze, c.1941

In 1941 the National Fire Service was formed so that fire forces could be concentrated where they were needed. Often firefighters travelled to other cities to assist during air raids.

Top left: Firefighters searching through debris for casualties, 1940s

The start of the Blitz saw the beginning of 57 consecutive nights of air raids. Auxilary Fire Service (AFS) firefighters worked alongside their regular colleagues to deal with the vast number of fires. The minimum age to join the AFS was 17. For 90 per cent of the auxiliary firefighters, this was their first experience of firefighting.

Below left: The aftermath of a V-1 flying bomb attack in Winchester Street, Pimlico, 1944

June 1944 saw attacks on London of a new kind. V-1 flying bombs and, later, the silent V-2 missiles caused mass destruction. The fire service experienced one of its busiest and most chaotic times.
The end of the war was announced in May 1945, leaving 327 of London's firefighters dead and more than 3,000 injured. The spirit of comradeship among firefighters and their dedication to their job were commendable. According to Winston Churchill the people of the fire service 'were a grand lot and their work must never be forgotten'.

Covent Garden

Right: Firefighters at Covent Garden Market fire, London, 20 December 1949

The fire occurred in the basement stores of the market and the first stations in attendance were Soho and Whitefriars. Firefighters entered the basement but many collapsed having lost their nose clips and been overcome by smoke. All attempts to place firefighters inside the building were stopped as the heat was too intense and it was decided to allow the fire to burn itself out. The Brigade gained control of the fire on 22 December, 50 hours and 30 minutes after the first call. In total 162 pumps and 850 firefighters attended. Station Officer Charles Fisher died and 66 firefighters were injured.

Smithfield

Left: Smithfield Poultry Market, London, 23 January 1958

In 1958 a very large fire took hold in Smithfield meat market. Described at the time as the worst fire since the Blitz, it was not stopped until the following day, and cooling down continued for two weeks. More than 450 pumps and 2,000 firefighters attended, of whom more than 40 were injured. Station Officer Jack Fourt-Wells and Firefighter Richard Stocking died as a result of getting lost in the market's maze of basement passages and storerooms and as a direct result a committee of inquiry was set up to look into the use of breathing apparatus (BA) and it recommended that a formal method of controlling BA at incidents be developed.

Dudgeons Wharf

Above: Dudgeons Wharf explosion, 17 July 1969

London Fire Brigade was called to attend a fire involving tank number 97 at Dudgeon's Wharf on the Isle of Dogs. Five firefighters: John Appleby, Trevor Carvosso, Terence Breen, Alfred Smee and Michael Gamble and one demolition worker; Reginald Adams were on the roof of tank 47. Two workers cut the bolts of the manhole cover at the bottom, when a huge explosion blew the roof off resulting in the deaths of all six men on top. The exact cause of the explosion was not clearly determined and as a result legislation was introduced. Known as the HAZCHEM code, the new rules strictly specified the practices to be followed in the removal of tanks that contained flammable substances.

Moorgate

Top left: Moorgate Underground crash, February 1975

At the peak of rush hour an underground train collided with the buffers on platform 9 of the Northern Line at Moorgate railway station. On the arrival of London Fire Brigade it could be seen that the three carriages of the train were badly compressed and that there were many trapped and injured people.

Firefighters from every station in London arrived in shifts and worked for five days in extreme heat, at times reaching 33C. There was such a high risk of infectious disease in these conditions that firefighters were inoculated before descending into the tunnel. It took five days to reach all of the victims. Forty two people lost their lives in the Moorgate crash, including the driver of the train.

Top right: Moorgate Underground crash, February 1975

This incident, being so far underground, rendered radio communications virtually useless and the Figaro communication system was used for the first time. The system was still in its experimental stage and had been designed by the Home Office to be used where walkie-talkies could not be. It operated on a medium wave frequency, enabling control and firefighters to relay messages between the tunnel and the surface.

King's Cross

Left: The King's Cross fire, 18 November 1987

A fire started on an escalator at King's Cross Underground station when a match or cigarette was dropped by a traveller. The fire rapidly spread to wooden panelling, paper advertisements and across the walls and ceiling, which were covered in flammable plastic materials. The fire erupted causing a flashover, spreading flames into the ticket hall above. It was intensified by the solvent-based paint that had been used on the station ceiling. Trains were still passing through the station and it is believed that this fanned the flames and spread the smoke.

More than 200 firefighters fought the blaze. The temperature was so intense that it caused the plastic leggings worn by the firefighters to melt to their legs and the intensity of the heat blew tiles from the walls and cracked solid concrete. Thirty one people died including Station Officer Colin Townsley.

The inquiry into the King's Cross fire lasted for six months and concluded with the production of the Fennell Report. This prompted the introduction of the Fire Precautions Regulations in 1989, ensuring that all escalators in subsurface underground stations were made from metal, and that automatic sprinklers and heat detectors in escalators be installed. Yearly fire safety training for all station staff and improvements in emergency services liaison were begun. There were many developments in London Fire Brigade as well. A new uniform was introduced, with jacket and trousers made from Nomex material, and a helmet with a full-face visor.

Left: Firefighters clearing debris, October 1999

At 8.11am on 5 October 1999 a Great Western Intercity train collided with a Thames Train at Ladbroke Grove. It was estimated that the trains collided at a speed of 120 miles per hour. 670 firefighters from 42 stations across London attended. The major incident involved overturned carriages and a fire on a section of a train, with smoke being seen across west London. Thirty-one people were killed and more than 520 injured. A report after the incident concluded that the crash was caused by signaling failures.

Above: Firefighters searching for casualties, December 1988

Two 12-coach commuter trains collided south of Clapham Junction railway station on Monday, 12 December 1988. A third empty train crashed into the wreckage, killing some of the survivors of the first crash. Crews used cutting gear to rescue trapped passengers. The Brigade worked with other emergency services to account for all the people. Thermal imaging cameras were crucial for locating trapped passengers. Thirty seven people died and 113 were injured.

The Hidden inquiry into the crash stated that the primary cause was wiring errors and British Rail work practices. The report made 93 recommendations for safety improvements, including a limit on the hours signalmen were allowed to work.

Left: Emergency services at Aldgate Underground station, 7 July 2005

On Thursday, 7 July four bombs were detonated on three tube trains and a bus during the morning rush hour, bringing devastation to the capital. Three bombs went off around 8.50am on underground trains just outside Liverpool Street and Edgware Road stations, and on another travelling between King's Cross and Russell Square. The final explosion was around an hour later on a double-decker bus in Tavistock Square. Fifty two people were killed.

'When we got to Tavistock Square there was a sharp intake of breath as we couldn't recognise what was in front of us. I made the decision to make an assessment of the scene by walking up to the bus; it was the longest walk I have ever taken'. Mick Ellis, Deputy Assistant Commissioner.

Emergency Planning

Left: Operation TEAL, 2014

A priority for London Fire Brigade is ensuring that London is prepared for a major incident. Working in partnership with other emergency services to develop strategic plans ensures a quick, efficient and coordinated response. The Emergency Planning Team work with the London Resilience Team and the London Emergency Services Liaison Panel. This is made up of representatives from the emergency services as well as local authorities. One of the largest exercises to test these plans was Operation TEAL, which took place in 2014. Over 220 emergency services personnel took part in a three-day exercise based on a simulated plane crash in the capital.

HazMat

Above: HazMat drill at Lambeth, 2012

Major incidents can include large-scale road or rail accidents, building collapse, flooding, terrorist attack or incidents involving hazardous chemicals. Highly specialised crews are on constant call to respond to chemical, biological, radiological and nuclear incidents. These teams can assemble huge shower structures to decontaminate hundreds of casualties exposed to a hazardous substance.

Urban Search and Rescue

Above and overleaf: Urban Search and Rescue demonstration, 2012

Urban Search and Rescue (USAR) teams are specially trained to deal with incidents such as building collapse. Using heavy lifting and cutting equipment, fibre optic cameras and listening devices they make structures safe and rescue victims. USAR also use search and rescue dogs to find survivors and provide first response medical aid to casualties, often in confined and difficult situations.

Extrication

Firefighters using hydraulic cutting gear at a road traffic accident exercise, 2012
London's firefighters are called to 10 road traffic accidents every day. The responsibilities of firefighters at this type of incident include protecting the scene of the accident to avoid further collisions, providing immediate medical assistance, securing the vehicle and casualties against any further movement, and safely removing injured passengers by using hydraulic cutting equipment.

Line Rescue

Line rescue exercise, 2012
The USAR team are trained to carry out line rescues using ropes to rescue people from tall buildings, cranes, or bridges.

Water Rescue

Left: Water rescue demonstration, 2012

The Brigade has a range of equipment which can be used to rescue people trapped by floodwater or in trouble in open water, rivers or canals. Specialist fire rescue units carry equipment such as inflatable boats. The Brigade also has dedicated flood response kits containing rigid flood rescue boats and paddles, dry suits, boots and pontoons for forming emergency bridges and walkways.

Fire Investigation

Above: Fire investigation team at an incident, 2014

In 1972 London Fire Brigade established one of the first fire investigation teams in the country. By 1984, the team had become a specialist unit and is now one of the most active teams of fire investigators anywhere in the world. The Fire Investigation Team, fire dogs, forensic scientists and scenes of crimes officers work together to reduce the risk of deliberate and accidental fires alike. With the knowledge of how and why fires start and spread, London Fire Brigade is better placed to make London a safer place to live, work and visit.

Fire dogs

Fire investigation dogs, Murphy, Roscoe and Sherlock, 2014

Since 2000, the Fire Investigation Team has trained fire dogs to recognise the presence of the 12 most common accelerants associated with arson, because dogs are more reliable and sensitive than most laboratory equipment. The fire dogs are selected at a young age for their enthusiasm, curiosity and a high drive for play. When investigating, the dogs wear protective boots and all live with their handlers.

Right: Community safety event, 2014

Community safety includes home safety visits, education in schools, reducing deliberately started fires and carrying out building inspections. This work helps people to stay safe from fires and other emergencies at work and in the home.

Home fire safety visits are an integral part of the Brigade's key aim to reduce accidental fires and injuries. Firefighters are trained to assess homes, offer advice and where appropriate, fit a smoke alarm.

Left: Schools Education Team in action, 2015

The Education Team provide free fire safety education to children in primary and secondary schools within the Greater London area. The team use their training and extensive experience to deliver key messages in a sensitive and reassuring way to over 100,000 schoolchildren a year.

Do you know your fire plan?

Ask your landlord or housing provider about the fire plan for your block and visit knowtheplan.co.uk for advice from London Fire Brigade.

Left: Know the Plan campaign poster, 2014

London Fire Brigade uses social media to successfully communicate with Londoners before, during and after incidents, as well as delivering serious fire safety messages. Successful campaigns have included the #takeawayworldcup campaign to tell football fans about the dangers of drinking and cooking.

The Know the Plan campaign is the result of the Lakanal House inquest. The campaign aims to provide advice to tenants and landlords living in and renting out purpose-built flats or maisonettes to ensure they have a clear understanding of what to do in the event of a fire.

London Fire Brigade cadets, Haringey, 2014

The Local Intervention Fire Education scheme began in Tower Hamlets in 2002. Thousands of people across London have since benefitted from intensive week-long courses designed to boost the self esteem of those taking part, by teaching them firefighting skills. This flagship youth engagement scheme has several teams across the capital working with 13 to 17 year olds from some of London's most deprived boroughs. The Brigade also runs the Fire Cadet programme and the Juvenile Firesetters Intervention Scheme, working with young people who have demonstarted fire setting behaviour.

As one of the largest fire and rescue services in the world, London Fire Brigade has been saving life and protecting property for 150 years, evolving and developing with an ever-changing capital. Firefighters, control officers and fire and rescue staff through years of hard work, perseverance and sacrifice have kept London safe in times of extreme adversity including two world wars, terrorist attacks and natural disasters to make our city a safer place to live, work and visit.

This book uses 150 photographs to illustrate 150 years of London Fire Brigade, providing a snap shot of our proud history.